Voices from the Fields

Children of Migrant Farmworkers Tell Their Stories

Interviews and photographs by S. Beth Atkin

Little, Brown and Company   Boston   New York   Toronto   London

To César Chávez, 1927–1993

❧

*To all the farmworker children and their families in the
Salinas Valley, whose lives have enriched mine invaluably*

❧

*And in memory of Betty Rudolph and Abe Shustick,
who in many ways made this book possible*

First Edition

Some names and identifying details of people in this book have been changed for reasons of privacy.
Francisco X. Alarcón translated "Hey Ése," "Home," and "Fieldworkers," as well as his own "The Promised Land," and reviewed all poetry translations. Enrique Degregori translated "The Strawberry," "After a Day in the Fields," "My Friends," and "My Mother." "My Parents" and "América Reyna, Bonita" were translated by the poets.

Library of Congress Cataloging-in-Publication Data

Atkin, S. Beth.
    Voices from the fields : children of migrant farmworkers tell their stories / interviews and photographs by S. Beth Atkin. — 1st ed.
        p.   cm.
    Includes bibliographical references (p. 96).
    Summary: Photographs, poems, and interviews with nine children reveal the hardships and hopes of Mexican American migrant farm workers and their families.
    ISBN 0-316-05633-2
    1. Children of migrant laborers — United States — Juvenile literature.   2. Children of migrant laborers — United States — Juvenile literature — Pictorial works.   3. Alien labor, Mexican — United States — Juvenile literature.   4. Alien labor, Mexican — United States — Juvenile literature — Pictorial works.   [1. Migrant labor.   2. Agricultural laborers.   3. Mexican Americans.   4. Children's writings.]   I. Title.
    HV741.A87   1993
    305.23'0896872 — dc20   92-32248

10 9 8 7 6 5 4 3 2

WOR

Published simultaneously in Canada by Little, Brown & Company (Canada) Limited

Printed in the U.S.A.

Contents

Acknowledgments

I would like to thank the children and their families who allowed me to use their poems, inverviews, and photographs in this book. In addition, many teachers, students, parents, and administrators helped make this book possible. Their constant dedication to helping improve the lives of Mexican farmworker children was a vital source of inspiration for me. I am grateful to all of them.

Thanks to: The Monterey County Migrant Education Office, for research, information, and reliable support; Liz Sanchez, Migrant Community Coordinator, Alisal Union School District, for researching and locating migrant students and giving her advice and time without hesitation; Maria González, Migrant Coordinator, Gonzales High School, for her diligent work locating students and their families; Raul Ramírez, Coordinator of Migrant Education, Alisal Union School District, for his support of and interest in my work with migrant students; Lenore Jiménez, Supervisor of Migrant Programs, North County High School District, for her support and kind encouragement; Rick Sandoval for advice on translating and referrals for community resources; Susan Ferriss and Fred Hernández, the *Monterey Herald*, for their interest and help with coverage of the Yo Puedo program; Emma Price, Alisal High School Day-care Center, for help with teenage mothers; Eliuth Machuca for help with translation; Cata Callaghan and Judy Baca, Sherwood Elementary School resource teachers, for their assistance in choosing appropriate students for this book; the Center for Community Advocacy for information on migrant labor camps; and Rhona Mahony for writing the initial proposal.

Thanks to the following people for photography support: Fred Blum for his excellent prints. Baron Wolman for all-around support and advice on photography and publishing; Tom Bentkowski for helping me believe that my photos for this project were worthy of publication; Fred Lyon for his gracious support; Jeff Bender for help with processing and printing; and Enrico Ferorelli for teaching me to always learn, have a sense of humor, and remain human while taking pictures.

My special thanks to the following people: Susan Baker and Amy Pofcher, both committed and talented bilingual teachers, for their constant dedication in assisting with interviews and photography, translating, and helping to find the inspiring children in this book. Working with them both kept my vision of this project intact. Raymond Isola, vice principal, Virginia Roca Barton School, for getting involved with this project and giving me the opportunity to work with the Yo Puedo program. The Yo Puedo program for giving me a better glimpse of the way in which Mexican migrant children want to improve their lives. The Yo Puedo poets featured in this book and their instructor, Patrice Vecchione. The instructors and participants showed me how their courage, dedication, perseverance, and warmth can change migrant children's lives. Francisco Jiménez for his kind and enthusiastic support of this book. Enrique Degregori for help with obtaining releases and translating poetry. Francisco Alarcón for use of his own poetry, for generously agreeing to translate poems, and for his warm support. All my loyal friends who have been generous and patient, especially after I chose to pursue a career in photography.

Lauren Adams, at Little, Brown, for her patient assistance through the book's completion. My editor, Ann Rider, for recognizing this project and encouraging me to write the text for this book. Her superb editing abilities, constant availability, and enthusiasm made its completion possible. My family, which has always taught me to look further and provided both the love and financial support to do so. David Marcus for believing in this project, helping with promotion, patient editing of text, and much more. And again to Amy Pofcher, who first told me about the lives of the Mexican farmworker children she teaches, gave me continual personal and professional support, and truly without whom this book would not have been possible.

Foreword ❧

This book gives a voice to the children of migrant farmworkers, our country's most exploited and deprived group of people. The poems and first-person narratives of Hispanic migrant children presented here speak with the voices of today's Hispanic migrant children as well as the collective voice of migrant children from many years past, including my own. Reading these testimonies and viewing the photographs that accompany them brought back many memories of my own childhood growing up in a family of migrant workers, from the time I was four until I was sixteen. I found myself reliving and sharing with these children many of the same feelings, thoughts, and reactions to the realities of migrant life. Tragically, our society has lacked the compassion and the will to eliminate some of these realities, which are as harsh and oppressive for the migrant children of today as they were for me thirty years ago.

Everything in this book is personal, full of life. The poems and interviews in this book relate life as it is experienced by these migrant children. They are living testimonies told in the children's words, often in their native language, Spanish. The Spanish text is accompanied by excellent English translations, which capture fine nuances of meaning. The telling of these stories is empowering, validating the importance of these children's experiences. Here we are not presented with sociological or scientific analysis and interpretations of migrant children's human condition — however valuable these might be. On the contrary, we are invited into the world of migrant children to listen to their own voices as they tell their stories. The total individual experiences they relate give us a mosaic of life that is tragic and hopeful, joyful and sad. We find "godliness" in every photograph, in every poem and interview. Stories by these children are nowhere else to be found.

Reading this book and reflecting on its profound meaning reminds me of W. H. Auden's call: "Clear away from your heads the masses of impressive rubbish. / Rally the lost and trembling forces of the will. / Gather them up and let them loose upon the Earth / 'Til they construct at last a human justice."

Francisco Jiménez
Associate Vice President for Academic Affairs, Santa Clara University

Introduction ❧

When I arrived in California from New York City and drove for the first time through the vast Salinas Valley, I was amazed by the great number of farmworkers and by the endless agricultural fields that surrounded them. I knew this was the part of the country that John Steinbeck had written about in *The Grapes of Wrath* and *East of Eden* and where so many of the nation's fruits and vegetables are grown. Broccoli, lettuce, onions, strawberries, raspberries, tomatoes, cauliflower, and asparagus are all harvested from these fields. But I knew very little about the people responsible for bringing these crops to our tables. Soon I learned that these workers are often migrant[1] and have no place to call home. I learned that they work long hours, often seven days a week, bending over to plant, pick, and pack fruits and vegetables. I discovered that their pay is minimal and that they support families that are much larger than the average American family of five. I wanted to get to know these people and see more of what their lives and the lives of their children are like.

Despite arduous working conditions, the workers were friendly when I approached them in the fields, and always willing to talk to me, even though they spoke little English and my Spanish was poor. I soon started visiting these fieldworkers in their homes. I found their families to be hospitable and touchingly open about their lives. Many parents, although proud of their Mexican heritage and language, candidly explained how they wished that their children would learn English. They spoke of their frustration over not being able to help their children with their homework because they themselves don't speak English, because they are uneducated, or because they return home late from the fields. In some families, the older children care for their younger brothers and sisters, helping them with their homework, as well as completing their own, because their parents work such long hours. One of the most disturbing yet also heartening situations I encountered were older siblings who chose to drop out of school to work in the fields so a younger sister or brother could finish school and improve her or his life. To me, this typified one of the many values of the Mexican farmworker family which I so admire: to help each other for the good of the entire family even at the cost of the individual.

But I found many situations in fieldworker homes both difficult to photograph and painful to hear about: ten children sleeping in one room and not attending school; parents not working because they had been injured working in the fields; families living on the verge of being evicted because they could not afford the rent; parents so tired that they

---

1. Workers are classified as *migrant* when they find employment in agriculture and live in temporary residences as a result of following the crops. *Seasonal* workers work in agriculture on a seasonal basis and usually settle in one area.

were unable to keep track of their children's attendance and progress in school; and parents keeping children out of school to work in the fields so they could help support the family.

Yet I also met children who are breaking their families' cycle of working in the fields and following the crops. Many of these children move less frequently than their parents and are legal residents of the United States. Many children don't work all week in the fields and often understand or speak English better than their parents. But I came to realize that the most essential difference between farmworker children and their parents is the children's chance to obtain an education. With support from parents, teachers, and migrant programs in their schools, many children are graduating from high school and even from college.

Migrant programs help students enroll in appropriate classes in their new school and qualify for special programs to maintain their correct school level. They help students get placed in bilingual programs, utilize health benefits, and find summer or part-time employment. The students enrolled are demonstrating great progress. In fact, the poems in this book were written by children while they were enrolled in migrant programs in the Salinas Valley. And the majority of these poets are now in college.

There are also special after-school and summer migrant programs in which students can learn additional skills. Migrant students can explore their heritage in the classroom by attending workshops in the history, music, art, and literature of Mexico. In addition, students who have attended migrant programs often stay involved by helping younger students or returning to become instructors. So new students have positive role models. They have the opportunity to meet the sons and daughters of migrant workers who are in or have completed college or who are professionals and are active in the Hispanic community. Thus children are shown how to change their lives through education without severing important ties to their own culture.

Some of the children in this book will find better lives than their parents. Others might continue to live their lives much as their parents have: with little education, in inadequate living conditions, moving their homes and families frequently, and working in the fields. But these children and their parents have also expressed their desire and hope for change. With the help of parents and teachers, Mexican farmworker children are speaking English, finishing high school, going on to college while proudly celebrating their roots. The voices of these children are resonating far beyond the fields where their families work, reaching to where their parents dream.

La Fresa
The Strawberry
❧

El trabajo de la fresa
es muy duro y delicioso
porque cuando uno la anda piscando,
uno va echando, una a la cajita
y dos a la boquita.

La fresa es de color muy rojo,
tiene forma de corazón,
que a uno se le antoja,
darle un buen mordidón.

La fresa es muy buena,
de sabor es dulce y sabrosa,
que niños y ancianos la comen
y hasta la gente golosa.

Ya se despide el fresero,
a cortar más fresitas,
para venírselas a traer
a estas lindas señoritas.

Otra vez se despide el fresero,
a cortar más fresas
y aunque con el lomo bien torcido
y hasta con dolores de cabeza.

Yo, ya me despido
porque yo no soy fresero
el lomo mío no estará torcido
porque yo soy un buen compositor.

Working in strawberries
is hard and delicious
because as you go along picking them,
you throw one in the box
and two in your mouth.

The strawberry is so deep red
and heart-shaped
that it makes you want to give it
a very big bite.

The strawberry is very good.
It's sweet and luscious.
Children and old people eat it
And people with a sweet tooth.

The strawberry worker says good-bye
to go and cut more little berries
so he can bring them
to those pretty girls.

The strawberry worker says good-bye
    again
to go and cut more berries
even though his back is twisted,
in spite of his headaches.

I say good-bye now
because I'm not a strawberry worker.
My back won't get twisted
because I'm a good writer.

Silvino M. Murillo

9

Working in *La Fresa*

◈

José Luis Ríos

Picking crops is very hard work. The hours are long and the positions uncomfortable and awkward. While some growers treat their workers well, others pay poorly, withhold earned pay, or do not adhere to pesticide and sanitary regulations. By coming in contact with crops that have been sprayed with pesticides as well as with pesticides that drift from nearby fields and from spraying planes, fieldworkers are exposed to hazardous chemicals and risk developing acute skin and eye problems, chronic headaches, and cancer. Despite these problems, fieldworkers generally keep a positive attitude. The pay is better than in Mexico, and obtaining work is uncertain, so migrant workers want to ensure that they and their families will be hired again.

Nearly 20 percent of all pickers are under eighteen years of age. Agriculture is the only industry in the U.S. that legally employs children under sixteen. Because families need the money and because parents have no one at home to take care of their children, young children are seen beside their parents picking crops, arranging strawberries in a box, or tying up packages of vegetables. If children are under the legal age limits (ten for strawberries and potatoes and twelve for all other crops), they are not considered to be working but rather "helping out."

Nine-year-old José Luis Ríos lives with his large extended family in a small house in Las Lomas, California. All of his relatives work in the fields, including his brothers and sisters. José Luis is often taken out of school to work alongside his family. The owner of the land where the Ríos family works has been charged by investigators of the Labor Department for violating some sixty provisions of the federal Migrant and Seasonal Agricultural Worker Protection Act.

❧ My name is José Luis Ríos, and I am in third grade. I have nine brothers and sisters. We live with our parents and aunt and uncle and cousins in Las Lomas. My grandparents live in Michoacan, Mexico. If they were here right now, I'd ask them to come and visit because I don't know them. My parents told me they used to work in the fields picking strawberries, garbanzos, lentils, and corn. All my relatives that I can think of work in the fields.

My parents work in *la fresa* [the strawberries] and *la mora* [the raspberries], and my mom sometimes packs mushrooms. During the week, they leave in the morning around six o'clock. I go and help them, mostly on weekends. I help pick the strawberries and put them in boxes. Last year my father took me to the fields a lot during the week, too, instead of bringing me to school. I would find out I was going because he would say, "Let's go pick strawberries now." I like going to the fields with my family because it is pretty out there.

The longest day in the field was when we picked a lot of strawberries. I felt bad and it was getting dark. We were out there so long. I said to my parents,

José Luis helping out in the strawberry fields

Taking a break with his father

"Let's go home," and finally they said, "We're going." It was hard to work so long. My body gets tired, and when it is muddy, my feet get covered with mud and it is hard to walk. Also, when it is muddy, my uncle has to park the truck far away, and I get tired and cold when I have to walk back to the truck.

My parents can't always find work. Usually there is work in the summer, so then I help my father every day in the fields. I have to pull up the grass around the strawberries, and I pick. I have to bend over. I bend over for a long time. When I work in the fields with my father, I eat strawberries and he gives me *frijoles* [beans] sometimes when we stop to eat. We rest, and then we go back to work.

13

Sometimes when I'm there, my aunt and uncle that live with us are in the fields working. My cousins are there, too. I play with my cousin Andrés. He is seven. I like to play with him because he is a *buena gente* [good person]. We play tag in the fields. My brothers work in the fields but not usually my sisters. They go to school. Rogelio, my little brother who's two, comes to the fields, but he just plays. He doesn't make any trouble.

When I work in the fields, I don't get paid. I don't want them to pay me because it's not good. They pay my parents for what I pick. I like that my parents get paid because then they buy me toy cars and trucks or maybe a bicycle. My brothers get paid. Ignacio is eighteen, and he works during the week. He doesn't

José Luis and his family

14

Joking with his brothers and cousin

go to school now, but he used to go to high school. Manuel is the oldest, and he works in the fields in Salinas. I want to work in the fields like my brothers when I'm older, because I can eat a lot of strawberries and out there you can watch the birds.

But sometimes it is hard and I'm tired in school on Mondays because I worked on the weekend. I also get a lot of bad headaches, so sometimes I have to leave school early or go and rest in the nurse's office. When my father took me to the fields last year during the week, it was hard to study when I got home because I was tired. It is hard to work and go to school at the same time.

I like coming to school better than working in the fields. I go to school on the bus at seven-thirty. I like going to school to learn because then you know things. If you don't know anything and you go somewhere and somebody asks you to

José Luis proudly displaying his Aztec school project

write something, you won't be able to. And when you're older you won't know anything. The people who haven't gone to school, they work in the fields.

I'm trying to learn English at school, but I like to speak Spanish because I'm understood better. I have more friends that speak Spanish than English. My parents tell me to study English, but I like studying the Native Americans best because they wrote, they did drawings, and they hunted buffalos. I like the Mayans. They made houses so the water couldn't get in when it rained. In school I like to write, too. I write about the birds because they are pretty and they fly. And I like to write about sheep and animals and also the Ninja Turtles.

When I get home from school, I have cookies. I eat most of my meals at school. My older brothers and sisters are there when I get home. They take care of me because my parents are working in the fields. My big sisters Carmela and Amelia help me with my homework and make cookies and coffee. Sometimes we take the strawberries from the fields home to eat. We make *fresa molida* — it's kind of a milkshake. Sometimes I take care of my little brothers and sister. I give them coffee and cookies. I have to watch out when I take care of them because cars come up our driveway and they could hit them. That's what happened to my little cousin. And sometimes we play right by the driveway. I play marbles with my brother Carlos and my cousin Jorge. I like to play hide-and-seek with my little sister Maria. My favorite place to hide is in the car.

When I'm bigger, I want to be a fieldworker and work in the strawberries because I like to work, and I want to do lots of other stuff. I would like to live for a time in Mexico, so I could know it. I would like to know my grandparents. I think it is different there, because there are more strawberries. If I had money when I'm older, I'd buy food, like milk, and other things. I don't want to have children when I grow up because I'll have to give them money. But if I did, I would want them to work in *la fresa*.

Hogar
Home
୬

Recuerdo la memoria
que un día fue real.
Veo mi cuarto flotar
al revés
en el fondo de mi mente.
Los muebles
no se quedan quietos.
Parece que se mueven
como si estuvieran vivos.
No puedo olvidar a mis padres
porque ellos son las personas
más importantes de mi vida.
Parece que me siguen
a dondequiera,
como si yo tuviera
el alma de ellos mismos.
Estoy de vuelta en mi cama y
la memoria se ha ido a volar.

I remember the memory
which was once real.
I see my room floating
upside down
in the back of my mind.
The furniture
does not stay still.
It seems to move
as if alive.
I can't forget my parents,
for they are the most important people
in my life.
They seem to follow me
all over,
as if I held their souls.
I am back in bed and
the memory has floated away.

Frank S. Pinedo

Always Moving

Julisa Velarde

Some farmworkers settle in one area and work seasonally, but many move continually all year round. They travel to follow the crops, or they work with one grower who supplies them work in several locations. Although Mexican migrant children today have more educational opportunities than their parents did, education is still often secondary to survival. When children migrate with their parents, they are pulled out of schools or they never attend them. Migrant programs can help children enroll in the correct classes and obtain the proper credits to continue in and graduate from school. They can help place them in jobs, direct them to counselors, and inform them of health aid available to migrants. But because these children move so frequently, they often either never enroll in migrant programs or cannot fully benefit from such programs, which might help them find a different life from that of their parents.

Twelve-year-old Julie Velarde moves about one to three times a year with her mother and younger sister. Sometimes, if their mother cannot take Julisa and her sister, they will live apart from her. But more often, they change schools and addresses. Julie is in the migrant program at the Salinas school she is enrolled in.

Ever since I was little, I have moved around. I was born in Blythe, California, and then we lived near Los Angeles and then in Nogales, Arizona, for a while. I don't remember a lot of places where we have lived or for how long we stayed. Now we mostly move from Salinas to Huron, California, or to Yuma, Arizona. My younger sister Christina and I have grown up moving around with my mom, but we don't work in the fields like she does. She has always worked in the fields. Even when we were still living with my father (he worked as a trucker), my mother would take me and Christina with her wherever she could get work. Now my parents are divorced, and my mom is the one who pays all our bills. To support us, she is always moving to find work in the fields. She works for lots of different companies picking lettuce.

When my mom goes away without us, we stay with my Aunt Mina or my Aunt Rosa. That way we don't have to keep moving so much. But, most of the time we go with her. It is hard for her to get work and take care of us and find someplace to live and everything. We live in different houses and with different relatives a lot. When we go to Yuma, we sometimes stay with one of my aunts, María Luisa or Elvira, or my uncle Daniel. If my mom has enough work and we stay long enough, sometimes we find our own house. I'm really lucky that I have my relatives to stay with. I always can talk with them. But I'd rather be with my mother.

Right now, I think she is coming back to take us up to Huron with her. She is looking for work there. I've been there before, but I don't remember it much or where we stayed. This time we will probably stay in different motels until we

Julie, Christina, and their mom, packed and ready for their next move

can find a house or an apartment. It depends if my mom is working there for a few weeks or a few months. A lot of times I don't know exactly where we are going or for how long.

When we move, sometimes I don't remember where I am. Once in Yuma, I woke up in the middle of the night, and I saw my aunt and I didn't know where I was. I was scared because I thought I was still in Salinas and I didn't know what she was doing there. To remember better where I am, I bring special things with me. Usually I only take the clothes and things that I really need. But I always take my teddy bear and a picture of all my family and ones of my cousins. Then I won't forget how they look and act. I have them write something on the back, and then when I come home to the new place, it is like seeing them. Because I miss them when I go.

I miss my cousin Amalia, who we live with sometimes in Yuma. I miss her a lot. Or my cousin Robert, who I was just living with here in Salinas. I miss him the most when I go, because if I'm depressed, he has a sense of humor and starts to tickle me when I say I have problems. I also have friends that I miss. Some of them help me and give me advice. But sometimes when I come back, they have moved, because their families are migrant, too. That's what happened with my friend Miriam, and now I don't see her anymore. My family stays in different places in Salinas, and sometimes when I come back to a place, my friends don't always remember me.

When I first came to Salinas, I think I was in third grade, or maybe fourth — I don't really remember, except when I first got to the new school, I didn't have anyone to hang around with. It's always hard that way. I think it is probably hard for my sister also, always making new friends, and getting used to new teachers and material in school like I do.

Sometimes the class is studying something higher in my school in Salinas and I have to catch up when I come back. Or the opposite, like when I was over there in Yuma in one school and we studied fractions. Then I came back here, and they hadn't done fractions yet. A lot of times the teachers don't help that much — they say they are busy with another student or something. They don't understand.

Going over homework with her teacher Mr. Chaney

Some are good, like my language arts teacher, Mr. Chaney. He takes time to see what the problem is. When you need a little bit more help, he is always there, and he is funny in class. I think he is really interested in helping us. But for me it is hard if the teacher doesn't listen to me, because I need help and I'm trying to catch up a lot.

Sometimes I tell my teacher that I'm leaving and she'll give me work for the stuff I'm going to miss. But sometimes we are gone for too long, and I have to go to a new school. I don't remember all the schools I've been to. But I know I would rather stay in one place and go to one school. I know that is what my mother would want, too.

My mother tells Christina and me that if we don't want to end up like her, we better go to school and get good grades. She helps me with my homework when she can and has always told me to learn English. I used to be real dumb in reading and writing in English. I hardly knew anything. They used to put me in classes that were in Spanish when I came to a new school. But my mom complained to my teachers and said that I could learn Spanish at home and that I needed to learn English at school. So I started to always take my classes in English. It was hard, but I learned by listening to the teachers talk in English, and I tried more and more to speak.

I speak English a lot now, like with my cousin Robert or in class and with my friends. Sometimes I talk with my friend Liz, who is in the migrant program, too.

We study a lot together, and in P.E. we practice frog stands in the pool. I like having her as my friend.

My mom says that I should keep studying hard in school and when I get older, get a good career and have a house of my own. That is what I would like to give her, a little trailer or a house that is all hers. I think that my sister and I should do our best in school so when we are older we'll have good jobs. Then we could take care of our mother so she doesn't always have to take care of us. Because now it is hard and we have a lot of bills and we are always moving around. Sometimes she wants to give us things and she can't because she doesn't have the money. She needs to save up for the bills. My sister and I understand that she can't buy us things. I feel sad because I know she wants to buy us things. If I could, I would snap my fingers to give her everything. I wish she had just one job that was easier than working in the fields, that she would always be here, and that we had one home.

Julie and her friend Liz after class

Después de un Día de Campo
After a Day in the Field
❧

Después de un largo, duro y caluroso día en el campo,
bajo los implacables rayos del Padre de la Vida,
mis músculos me duelen y mis huesos parecen
quebrarse como si fueran cristales.
Estoy sucio, sediento y con hambre.
Mi cuerpo está muy cansado y adolorido
que temo que se derrumbe
como un viejo edificio que está siendo destruido.

After a long, hard, and hot day in the field,
under the implacable rays of the Father of Life,
my muscles ache and my bones hurt and crack
as though they were crystals breaking.
I'm dirty, thirsty, and hungry.
My body is so tired and sore
that I fear it might crumble
like an old building being torn down.

Eugenia Ortiz

My Home

&

Manuel Araiza

Many children of fieldworkers live in homes that are not only overcrowded but also poorly ventilated and without heat. Toilet, bathing, and eating conditions in both migrant labor camps and private housing are often unsanitary. Nutrition is often inadequate, and the water contaminated from pesticides in the nearby fields threatens families with typhoid, infectious hepatitis, and dysentery.

Even if parents are aware of the hazards that surround them, most need the work and cannot find or are not eligible for low-income housing. They are often uninformed of migrant programs that can help improve their families' health and living conditions. Or sometimes families do not utilize services because they are constantly moving, or are undocumented and fear deportation. Most farmworker children have never known a decent standard of living. If these children continue to work in the fields and do not alter their living conditions, their average lifespan will be forty-nine years, compared with the average American lifespan of seventy-three.

Ten-year-old Manuel Araiza, who has often worked with his parents in the fields, lives in a one-room home with his family of eight near Castroville, California. Shortly after this interview was taken, the county, citing numerous health violations, ordered the owner of the property to evict his tenants and not replace them.

When I was five, my whole family came here, over the hills, across the border. It was night. We paid someone to take us. A coyote — that is someone who takes you over the border. I don't know how much you pay him. I felt bad when we went over the hills, scared, too. We walked and walked all night, and then we got into a car that the coyote had hidden. We got in the back, the very back of the car, and he took us to Tijuana. My father picked us up there in another car. I wasn't scared to go in that car because I was with my father.

I used to live in Aguacalientes, Mexico. My mother would come to the U.S., without us, to visit my father. He was up here working in the fields when I was born. Since he had never visited us in Mexico, I didn't really know him when we came to California to live with him.

We first lived in a trailer with two rooms. Then we moved to this house. They are both smaller than our house in Mexico. That house was pink and it had two floors. Our house here is one room with a kitchen. I liked the house in Mexico better because it had bunk beds. Now I sleep with my brother, Juan, and my father in one bed. My mother and my sisters, Bertha, Fatima, Cristina, and Carla, sleep in the other one. Since it is a small place, we are all squished together, and sometimes it is really hot. It was hot in Mexico, but it is worse here because there is only one window and it doesn't open and close so well. Then in the winter it is sometimes cold inside. We don't have heat.

The room where Manuel and his family sleep

We used to have a bathroom in our house in Mexico, but here the bathroom is outside. One room has a shower and one has a toilet. We share them with the other families on the property. I think there are about eleven or twelve families. But my family is the biggest. My friend Benja lives next door. He has five people in his family, and their house is the same size as ours. It would be better if all the families had bigger places to live. They would be more comfortable. Because there are too many people living on the land, the inspector came and told the owner that all the people have to move. He also said there were too many families sharing the three bathrooms, and he said we didn't have a furnace for heat.

Manuel and his sisters just outside their house

If we have to move, I hope that I still have room to play outside. Now I play on the weekends or after school if my parents don't take me to the fields with them. Sometimes they come from work to get me at home after school, and they take me to the fields. They work hard in the lettuce, strawberries, raspberries, and flowers. Juan and Fatima go also, but Bertha stays home to watch my little sisters. We help my parents in the fields. I like to arrange the strawberries in the box after I pick them. It gets very hot sometimes when I'm out there. So I have juice or I drink water from the little wood house in the fields, where you can wash your hands.

I don't always go to the fields after I get home from school. Sometimes I study. I like to read. My favorite book is about *camiónes* [trucks]. I got it from the free book program. I made a book in summer school about trailers and one about a mouse, but the mouse had to move at the end because he got thrown out of his house. He moved to a big house made of grass.

Looking after his baby sister, Carla, in their kitchen

I like going to school here more than in Mexico. Here, they don't make you go home if you do something bad. In Mexico they didn't give you anything to eat at school. My mother had to bring it to me. Now I get breakfast and lunch. My favorite thing to eat at school is macaroni and cheese. At home my favorite is *arroz con pollo* [chicken with rice]. Sometimes my parents bring strawberries or lettuce home from the fields for us. I eat lettuce sandwiches at home and *frijoles* [beans] and cactus. I don't eat candy much. I used to have trouble with my teeth. They were always falling out and breaking. But I went to the dentist and I think they are O.K.

Here, they make you wait for a long time at the dentist and the doctor. I had to go to a lot of doctors for my ears. They made me walk around a lot to see all of them. My father took me because the nurse at school told me to go. My ears hurt, but if I put my hands over them, it made them stop hurting. So I always slept that way. The doctor gave me pills, but as soon as I took them my head started hurting so I stopped taking them.

Now I feel better, but I hope we don't have to move. I'll miss my friends at school, like Rodolfo and Benja. And then I'll have to make new ones. But if we do move, I'd like to live in a bigger house with gardens in back. I'd like that when I get older. I want to work in the fields and pick the raspberries and take them in a truck to the store and drive my truck all over America. I could go really far and sleep in the truck because right behind the seat is the bed. I'd also like to learn how to make houses. That would take a lot of studying. And my parents are always telling me to study. Because when you get big you are not going to get work if you haven't studied. My teacher told me that, and my father. So, if I don't study, then maybe I won't get work and have money to buy my parents a blue car or a house.

Manuel with his best friends in the school playground

Mis Amigos
My Friends
ᔰ

Mis amigos,
estrellas que cubren el cielo.
Ellos me escuchan
con sus manos en sus corazones.
Ellos me ayudan como si yo fuera
el diamante más precioso.
Ellos me entienden,
como yo entiendo
los consejos de mi madre.
Ellos me aconsejan fácilmente
como que una nube es blanca.

Mientras tanto mis no-amigos
me ignoran como a un perro y me critican
como a una flor marchita.

My friends,
stars that cover the sky.
They listen to me
with their hands on their hearts.
They help me like the most
precious diamond.
They understand me,
like I understand
the advice of my mother.
They give me advice
like the white of the clouds.

While the no-friends
ignore me like a dog
and criticize me
like a withered flower.

Claudia García Moreno

Fitting In

❧

Andrea Martínez

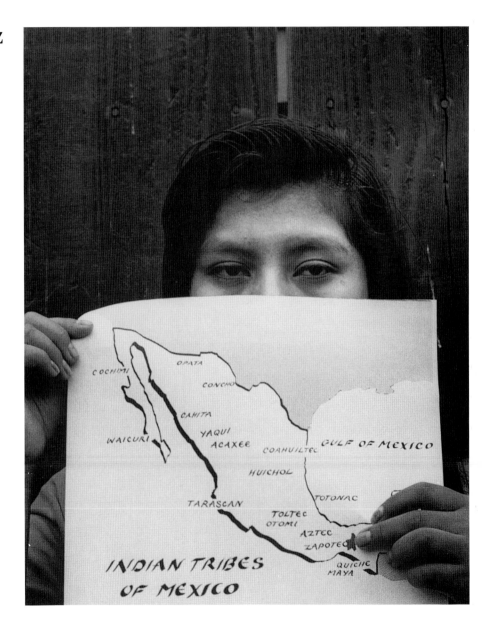

Children of Mexican migrant workers often grow up feeling torn between American culture and their Mexican heritage. Many of them go back and forth to Mexico, and with friends and family in both countries, they straddle two different worlds.

Although schools such as those in the Salinas Valley often have a large Mexican migrant student population, many children still feel they are discriminated against. When they arrive from Mexico, they are frequently placed below their level in classes. Often this is due to the language barrier, but many students sense they are treated differently simply because they are Mexican.

Eighteen-year-old Andrea Martínez, a Zapotec Indian from Oaxaca, in southern Mexico, spoke neither Spanish nor English when she moved to the U.S. several years ago. She was not only isolated from her family and the Zapotec language but also ostracized by schoolmates because she did not speak Spanish.

ﺮ I am from El Mirador, a village near the town of Ojitlan, by the city of Tuxtepect, in the state of Oaxaca, Mexico. I am a Zapotec *india* [Indian]. Zapotec is a kind of *indígena* [native] group from Mexico. The dialect we speak is Zapoteca. My grandparents are Zapotec and were born on the *ranchito* [small ranch] I lived on, and they worked off the land, planting seeds, harvesting the crops, and selling them if there was extra. My mother grew up there also. My real father was from around there, too. But I never really knew him. My grandmother raised me so my mother could work in Mexico City.

I started working on the *ranchito* when I was eight, harvesting chilies, corn, and coffee. Lots of children did the same. There were about fifty families living in our community then. Everyone had their own land, which had been divided up by a committee. The committee was also supposed to collect money for the school. But most of the parents said the school didn't work. They preferred their children to work in the fields instead of studying. Many people where I grew up thought that if you are a girl, you are just supposed to get married. That is what my grand-

Andrea and Francisco, happy to have their mother home

mother thought, so I worked, and my brothers went to school. My grandmother told me, "Since you are a girl, you are not supposed to study." She thought that girls were lowly. So as you can see, I have known discrimination since I was small. Another way I've known it is growing up in Mexico and being Zapotec. Even though we come from the same blood, the Mexicans would discriminate against us because we were Indian. They would say, "Indio, get to work." That is because we are poor, and we had to work hard.

I moved to the Salinas Valley four years ago with my mother and my brother Francisco. My brother Sergio stayed in Mexico. I have a little sister, also, named Marilyn. She was born here just a year ago. My stepfather, who is her father, came with us from Mexico, too, but I didn't know him because my mother met him after she left the *ranchito*. My mother first worked here mostly in the grapes. But now I don't get to see her much because she works a lot in Yuma, Arizona, in *la lechuga* [the lettuce]. It's difficult, and every day I miss her. When we first moved I felt alone here. My mother would leave to work, and it was really hard because my stepfather only speaks Spanish. I couldn't talk to him because I only spoke Zapoteca. Where I grew up, the only time I ever heard Spanish was when an outsider came and someone would talk in Spanish out of need. If someone spoke to us in Spanish, we were afraid because we didn't understand what they were saying. We were also embarrassed that we couldn't talk back to them.

Everything here was different from where I grew up: the food, the people, the clothes. But the hardest part for me when I moved was the language. I couldn't speak Spanish, and I didn't know English. Also no one in my community in Mexico knew how to write or even how to pick up a pencil. My mother told me that things would be better soon because here at least I could get an education.

There is nothing similar about Zapoteca and Spanish, and it took me a year just to learn Spanish. My stepfather talked to one of my teachers and explained

Andrea taking care of Marilyn with her stepfather

that I didn't know Spanish. In my Spanish class the teacher had her aide help me a lot. Little by little, she taught me how to make sentences. But learning English was harder. I stayed in the same level for two years. The English class had all Mexicans, and I had a classmate who tried to help me a lot. She is still my friend. But she only spoke Spanish, and so I didn't really understand. In other subjects, I was put in classes that were too advanced for me because I didn't know the language. Like in social studies: the teacher told me I should raise my hand more in class. She knew that I had the answers, like the capitals of countries in Central America. But I didn't know how to say the answers. So I stayed after school, and

Andrea listening to her mother while holding Marilyn

she helped me. Then I advanced in the class and got an A. I was lucky because a lot of teachers helped me.

My mother encouraged me a lot when she was home. I didn't know how to defend myself, and she helped me. She told me to try to speak in Spanish and not to quit even though the students were making fun of me. They pulled my hair and they called me a *mensa* [fool]. They insulted me. The *pochas* especially — their parents are from Mexico but they were born here and speak mostly English. They think they are great and that once they know a little English they are *gabachas* [*gringos*, non-Mexicans]. They called me *"india"* to insult me because that is what they call people who just came from Mexico. But what they didn't know is that I am a true Indian.

For me, the *pochas* are worse than the *gabachas*. The time I went on a field trip, for the FBLA [Future Business Leaders of America], everybody treated me really well. They weren't Mexican, and when I told them I couldn't speak English well, they said, "Andrea, you can speak very well." I've also taken an English literature class, and no one American made fun of me. But I know that some Mexicans here have problems and are treated badly. In King City, which is right nearby, some high school students want a school newspaper in Spanish, but the school won't let them have it. So maybe it is easier here for Americans than Mexicans. But I'm not sure because I usually don't see what problems Americans confront, only the ones Mexicans have. What I do think is Americans educate their children better.

The hardest problem for Mexicans is that they need to know English to live here. They have a hard time knowing only Spanish. But most of them have had an education in Mexico. There are not a lot of students who have had to face what I did. It's not that I'm the only one, but when I moved to the United States, I hadn't gone to school, and I couldn't communicate at all.

Now things are better because I have friends. Before if some girls would walk by me and say, "Hi. How are you?" I was too embarrassed to talk to them in Spanish. I was afraid. Now I'm not. Also, since I've come here I have had the opportunity for an education and I'm learning a lot. One of the best experiences

I've had is going to the Yo Puedo [I Can] program. It is a special summer program at a college campus in Santa Cruz that helps children of migrant workers. It motivates them to go forward and improve their lives. A lot of people helped me with the Yo Puedo application, and I got in. Just getting accepted gave me more confidence because I never thought I would. Nobody made fun of me there, and being at a university was really nice. The program helped me in many ways. I learned computers there, and now I want to become a computer engineer when I go to college. It also made me more comfortable to be in the United States.

Now that I have finished the program, I'm still learning through Advanced Leadership Training sessions. Once a month, all the Yo Puedo students teach little migrant children to try hard and be motivated in school. I tell them to never quit school. We have workshops and do skits on subjects like self-esteem, language barriers, and discrimination. One day I will stand up and speak at a workshop on discrimination. Because the kids in the program should see that it's not just the Americans that discriminate against us but also Mexicans who are born here, the

Instructing younger migrant students in a self-esteem workshop

Andrea and friends at a Yo Puedo Advanced Leadership Training workshop

pochas, who discriminate against other Mexicans, too. I don't want to offend them but I would tell them, "You will know what it is like when you go to university and feel discrimination, because Americans will see you as Mexican." Then maybe they will notice that discrimination is everywhere.

Since I have been here for a while, I now know what it feels like to be Mexican. I speak Spanish and have friends that are Mexican. But I still think my Zapotec heritage is important. I don't speak my dialect much, because my mother isn't around. But I try to think about it by myself. It is important not to lose it, because it is in my blood. If I had to choose between being Mexican and Zapotec, I'd choose both. Because I can't discriminate against Zapotecas, my people.

Mis Padres
My Parents
ॐ

Ustedes
mis queridos
que pendiente
de mí siempre están

Escucho
ésas sus palabras dulces
sus consejos buenos
que siempre me dan

Escucho
la puerta por las mañanas
cuando al trabajo
ustedes van

Los miro cuando regresan
cansados y agitados
de tanto trabajar

Ustedes
son como los pájaros
que siempre volando van
dentro de mi corazón

You
my dear parents
always worry
about me

I hear
your sweet words
your good advice
that you always give me

I hear
the door in the mornings
when you are on your way to work

I see you when you come home
tired and exhausted
from so much work

You are
like the wonderful birds
that are always flying
inside my heart

Adriana Ochoa

45

My *Familia*

≥•

Victor Machuca

A Mexican child has a very different sense of the importance of family than do many American children. Mexican children speak with respect about their grandparents and parents, and most children want to contribute to their family somehow. They help by working and caring for the younger children. Because parents work in the fields and often have little education, they rely on their older children to help the younger ones in school and to be positive role models. Because the needs of the family are stressed more than those of the individual, parents trust that when their children improve their lives, the whole family will benefit.

Fifteen-year-old Victor Machuca came to the U.S. just over three years ago. Like many Mexican and Mexican-American children, he speaks of the vital role of his older siblings and of the strong bonds and values of his family.

I came to California from Cuernavaca, Morelos, in Mexico. My parents both come from very big families. I have twenty-three aunts and uncles and forty cousins. But my immediate family is small. There is my mother, father, and my sisters, Eliuth, who is twenty, and María Cruz, who is eighteen. I'm fifteen. My father used to work in the fields in Mexico. He planted rice there. He works in the fields here, and when he can't find work, he does construction. My mother used to work here in *el tapeo de garlic* [the garlic harvest], but right now she is working in a carrot cannery. Since my parents didn't always have a lot of work, they didn't want to have a lot of children. They wouldn't be able to support them. I am close to my sisters and parents because they are my family and I have a right to be united with them.

My relatives are close because of their friendship. Most of my father's relatives lived in the same town in Mexico as we did. That is why we are closer to my father's family, like my grandparents. I respect them because they are older and because my parents have always shown me to have respect for them. Like my father does. He remembers them a lot now that he is in the United States, and he sends them money when he has extra. When I lived there and we went to visit

Victor and his family enjoying dinner together

them, they always received us well. We would fish at the river near their house. The memory I have of them is that whenever I fought with anyone, they told me that I had to fix the problem with the person I was fighting — that I shouldn't rely on them to solve it. I always remember that, and now if I have a problem, I work it out with that person and not my parents.

I only saw my grandparents on my mother's side twice a year. I remember that if anything ever happened to me, they helped me. When we did go to visit them, in Guerrero, we would ride on their donkey. Also I would help them in their orchard planting things. I liked to learn from them, like digging a bowl around the plants to keep the water in. Their orchard had banana, mango, papaya, and plum trees. When they came to visit us, they would always bring us things, like bread and their fruit and *cariño* [affection]. All my grandparents are important to me. But since we came to the United States, I don't see them much.

Now we only see my family in Mexico on long vacations. I'd like to visit them more, like my uncles and aunts. Every year we always celebrated Christmas with them in our house. There, in Cuernavaca, we owned our house, and there was room for all our family. Here, it is too expensive to own a house, and we don't exchange presents or prepare a special meal, like we did there. My favorite was the

Relaxing in the fields with Eliuth and María Cruz

49

Christmas meal. It wasn't like an everyday meal. We had *posole*. It's corn cooked with *carne* [meat] and chili powder. My mother made tamales, sweet and chili, and we had a peach *atole* — it's a sweet milk dessert with rice. The whole family was there. All my father's relatives and some of my mother's. There were at least twenty of us. Here just my parents, sisters, and I celebrate, but simply, because sometimes we don't have enough money.

My family and I still do things together here; they are just different things from what we did in Mexico. When we first moved here, we all worked together. We worked in the *cebollitas* [green onion] fields. We worked as a family because it's faster. We helped each other. One person pulls the onion out of the ground, the other person shakes it, another cleans it, and then one of us ties them up together. I think doing things like working together is important. It makes our family stronger. Sometimes we stay home and I help my father work on our car. We try to eat dinner together, and when my parents aren't working too late, we go to church together. But my favorite thing to do with them is to go to the park to feed the ducks.

My parents don't think I should work in the fields when I get older. They tell me that I shouldn't lose a career like a lot of people in the fields. They've also told me that some people get sick because of the work they do in the fields. I think that they tell me these things for my well-being, so that I'll study and finish high school.

They say it would be good to go to college. My mother always says she wants me to be a doctor. My father says that if I don't become a doctor, I should become an architect. Most of the time, I think I would like to be a doctor to save people who are sick and to try to help people who need help. Sometimes though, I think I'd like to become a lawyer. I would help people get their papers and then people, like my family and others I know, could cross *la frontera* [the border] from Mexico, legally, instead of risking their lives crossing mountains.

My parents would like me to go to college, but they don't tell me that I have to. One reason I want to go to college is that I admire Eliuth and María Cruz because they are both in college here and they speak English well. I would like to be at their level of English, but I didn't learn how to conjugate the verbs in junior

50

Feeding ducks at the park — Victor's favorite family activity

high. I think I'd prefer to go to college in Mexico, because of the language and it's faster there. It's also very expensive here. My sisters tell me not to quit and that I should keep trying with my English, and that if I go to college here, maybe I can get migrant scholarships like they have.

My sisters have always helped me and given me advice. When I was little, they took care of me when my parents were working. If something happened to me, like if I fell down, they cured me. I have good memories of them taking care of me. If anything ever happened to my parents, I would work and try to take care of my sisters. But I know they would encourage me not to fall behind in school just to help them. I know they would try to help me, too. When we are older, if my sisters have children and visit me, I would treat them well. I would give them food and help them if they needed to go somewhere. I would always help them and my parents.

The Machuca family

For example, when my parents get older, if they can't work, I'll help them. They always help me and have given me food since I was little, so I would like to do the same for them. Sometimes now I would like to be able to give them money. If I was making, let's say, fifty dollars a week, I would give all the money to them and they would give me back what I needed.

I think my friends feel like I do about their families. Their parents are important to them, and they listen to their advice. I have some friends that do not respect their family. Their parents tell them that they don't like their kids to smoke, but they smoke anyway. I listen to my parents, because they always give me good advice. If I ever have children, I would want them to listen to my parents also. I would want them to respect their grandparents.

When I get older, I want to live close to my family, all of them. There isn't anything more important than my family. I feel an obligation to be with them, not because they tell me to but because I feel this. It is my own will to be with them. They help me in everything, and they are the only family I have.

Hey Ése
To all the gangs

Tú, con tu alma sweet y sincera,
tú, que dentro de ti hay un niño que llora
and needs to be calmed

De ti dicen varias cosas, but they don't
*   know you,*
you are not mean, ése, yo lo sé
tú eres especial,
disculpa si algun día te he ofendido,
pues ignoraba la sencillez que existe
en tu corazón.

You fight por tu bienestar
así como un águila pelea por su libertad
Eres bueno, eres romántico, y cuando tú
*   expresas*
lo haces from the bottom of your heart.

He descubierto que ahora te admiro,
que eres tan alto como una estrella,
y tan brillante como una de ellas.
Para mí significas dulzura,
you mean peligro to me,
pero también significas dulzura.

Eres mi cholo admirado ése,
your sweetness makes me feel
"chiquita" de corazón.
I hope one day tú entiendas
que soy una amiga que te admira
y además te da la razón.

You, with your sincere and sweet soul,
you, who carries a child crying inside of
    you
and needs to be calmed

They say things about you, but they
    don't know you,
you are not mean, *ése*, I know
you are special,
sorry if one day I offended you,
because I didn't know the simplicity
    that exists
in your heart.

You fight for your well-being
the way an eagle fights for its freedom,
You are kind, romantic, and when you
    express yourself,
you do it from the bottom of your
    heart.

I have found that I now admire you,
you are as tall as a star,
and as bright as one of them.
To me you mean sweetness,
you mean danger to me,
but also you mean sweetness.

You are my admired *cholo*, *ése*,
your sweetness makes me feel
"very small" in my heart.
I hope one day you understand
that I am a friend who admires you
and also thinks you are right.

Leticia Orozco

Life in a Gang

ઢ

Frank Rosas

Gangs and gang-related violence are growing problems in the U.S. In Salinas, California, the largest city in the Salinas Valley, there are at least thirty gangs. Members' ages range from nine to twenty-six. Gangs are prevalent among the valley's Mexican and Mexican-American teenagers, who find support in the gangs that they join in the U.S. But gangs such as the two major Mexican ones, the Norteños [Northerners] and Sureños [Southerners], often fight each other.

Seventeen-year-old Frank Rosas moved to the U.S. three years ago. Six members of his family live here also, with one sister and brother still living and working in the fields in Mexico. After attending several new schools, Frank joined a Sureño gang. One of the many definitions of the gangs in Frank's neighborhood is that Norteños tend to speak English within their gang and are usually Mexican-Americans who were born in the U.S. or have lived here for a long time. Sureños are proud to speak Spanish, often know little English, and are usually recent immigrants to the U.S. from Mexico.

Eighteen years ago, my father started coming to California to work in the fields. He would come for six months and then go back to Mexico. He works in irrigation in *la lechuga* [the lettuce]. When my mother was pregnant with me, my parents came here together from Mexico, so I would be born here and could be an American citizen. Everyone else — my six brothers and sisters and my parents — were all born in the state of Jalisco, Mexico. When I was a baby, my mother and father went back there with me. That's where I lived until I was fifteen.

The first time I entered the U.S., my father brought me here to get my passport. At the border, they made it difficult and didn't want to let me through. They didn't believe that I was born here, and I didn't have any identification. I didn't speak English, and I didn't know the national anthem. Even though I am American because of my papers, I have always considered myself Mexican because my parents are Mexican. I've always believed in Mexico. I've never felt like I was from here.

I've lived in Watsonville, Salinas, and Soledad since I've moved to California. In each place, I went to a new school, and they kept changing the grade I was supposed to be in. I started out in ninth grade, and now a year and a half later, I've been placed in twelfth at a high school in Gonzales, which is near Soledad. It was hard to get used to the different grades they kept putting me in, but the main difference for me between school here and in Mexico is the gangs. There was nothing harmful in school in Mexico, and there weren't any fights or gangs.

Even though there were some gangs at my school in Watsonville, I liked that school a lot. There weren't fights that often, and my teachers helped a lot, especially with my English. It was difficult for me to leave there because it was the first American school I went to. It was where I met my first friends in the U.S. Then

Frank's family in their home

I went to school in Salinas. I was with my brother and we got along with everyone. I know there are some gangs there, like the L.P.T.'s [La Posada Trece], but we didn't have any problems with them. But here at Gonzáles, I have had some problems with gangs.

When I first started going to Gonzáles High, I started hanging out with some *compañeros* [buddies, classmates]. We weren't a gang or anything like that — we just spent time together and helped each other with our homework. But after a while this gang at school, the North Side Gonzas, said that we were a gang, and they started looking for fights with us. So then we formed a gang, the V.L.K.'s [Los Verdes Latinos Kings]. We started to defend ourselves, and we forgot about school. If the North Side Gonzas hadn't bothered us, I wouldn't have been in a gang at all.

Our gang started differently than most. Usually if you want to be a gang member, you tell the gang you are alone and there are others trying to fight you. After that, if they make you a gang member, they do something like an initiation, called jumping. Usually they take you to a house, and they beat you up for a few minutes. You can't defend yourself — you have to endure it, and when they finish, they give you a name like Snoopy or El Payaso [the Clown]. That is my name.

Most things about being in a gang are bad, but there are some good things, too. It is good to be able to talk to or get advice from your gang. Before we were a gang, I was hanging out with this group of friends to relieve me from the pain I had. My family had a problem because my dad was with another woman. So I looked for friends to talk to and I really trusted one friend in this group. I think that's one of the reasons people join gangs. Some need more affection or their dad drinks a lot and fights with their mother. They have problems at home, so they join a gang. But some join just to defend themselves better or so they can use drugs and liquor.

It is easier to get drugs when you are in a gang. I tried drugs but didn't like them. I don't think I would have if I hadn't been in the gangs. I told the gang members that I didn't like them using drugs, so they stopped, at least in front of me. Some gangs sell drugs, and sometimes they steal car stereos or money from

On a neighborhood wall covered with gang grafitti

stores, but they never steal from houses. Almost everybody in a gang has a weapon. I think it makes them feel more secure. Some have guns, but the most common weapon is a *navaja* [switchblade, knife].

The worst thing about gangs is when they kill someone. A gang in Salinas shot a guy when he walked by. He had a red bandana in his pocket (red is the Norteño color) and he told them he was Norteño when they asked him, and he flashed a fourteen, the signal for the Norteños. They were all Sureños, thirteens, so they shot him. Not all gangs kill, but the majority of gangs, like mine, are known as fighters.

I didn't want to fight, but I felt safer in the gang. Our gang usually just walked around or rode our bikes. Some of the members wrote grafitti on the walls. They draw their "13" design. We didn't fight as much as other gangs, but at school there wasn't any other way to defend ourselves. We did look for help at school, but it was too late. The migrant program talked to us and gave us advice. Some of it was helpful and some wasn't. They told us to behave well, to disband, and to not pay any attention to the other gang when they started a fight. We followed that advice, but we got tired of the other gang saying things about us, so the fights began again. We wanted to listen to them but we couldn't. We were already in too deep.

One day, this *cholo* [guy] from the North Side Gonzas, who was always looking for a fight with me, walked by me in the school and started a confrontation. He said I was looking for a fight, and I told him that he was the one who wanted to fight. Then when I asked him who he wanted to fight, he said, "All of you." So about fifteen of us ended up fighting, and the police came to stop us. And after the fight the principal called my father and told him I should leave school and go on independent study. He thought the gang might shoot or stab me, so it would be safer if I was out of school. My father agreed, and I think he made the right decision for me.

I'm glad that I'm not in the gang anymore. I didn't have a problem when I left. Normally leaving is just like when you enter, but uglier. The whole gang comes to beat you and they leave you lying on the ground. Even though I'm not in a gang anymore, I will always be considered part of the gang by other people. I was supposed to go back to school, if the problem passed, but the school hasn't told me anything.

So I'm still on independent study. In the afternoons, I go during the week to a class near where I live. Also, I work every day with my brother José, doing landscaping. I used to have a lot of *ganas* [desire] to study. Before, my parents always told me to "put more desire," or try harder, when I was studying. So I did, and my grades had gone up to A's and B's at Gonzáles. But now it is harder to study without being in class — the material is not the same, and the teachers who are supervising don't help as much as at Gonzáles. So now I'm not so sure it will be as easy to graduate and get the career I want. I used to think about my future. Now I don't have dreams about getting where I thought I would.

Frank and his little sister, Eunice, playing with their niece

Hanging out with one of the guys from his old gang

I think gang violence is a big problem now. It is only getting worse, and something should be done to stop it. For example, they shouldn't show only violence on TV or in movies. I think they should show the opposite and tell you how to get out of gangs and not use drugs and kill people. If I could, I would take every gang and throw them in jail and punish them to give them a lesson. I would have them do hard work so that they calm down and stop being in gangs. Because being in a gang isn't good for your future. Instead of helping you, they harm you.

Mi Madre
My Mother
ی&

Tú, madre divina
que nunca conocí,
no pude sentir tu amor
ni tu cariño de madre.

En mi alma hay un dolor,
un dolor muy profundo
que siempre llevo conmigo
a donde quiera que voy.

Tú, madre adorada
que diste vida
y no tuviste la oportunidad
de tenerme en tus brazos.

Madre mía,
llevo conmigo una imagen,
una imagen tuya que no olvidaré
que llevo en mi alma.

You, my divine mother
who I never knew,
I was not able to feel your love
nor your motherly affection.

In my soul there is a pain,
a very deep pain that I always carry
   with me
wherever I go.

You, my adored mother
who gave me life
but not the opportunity
to be held in your arms.

My mother,
I keep with me an image,
your image that I will never forget
that I keep in my soul.

Celia Camarena

Away from
Home

&

Jesús Rodríguez

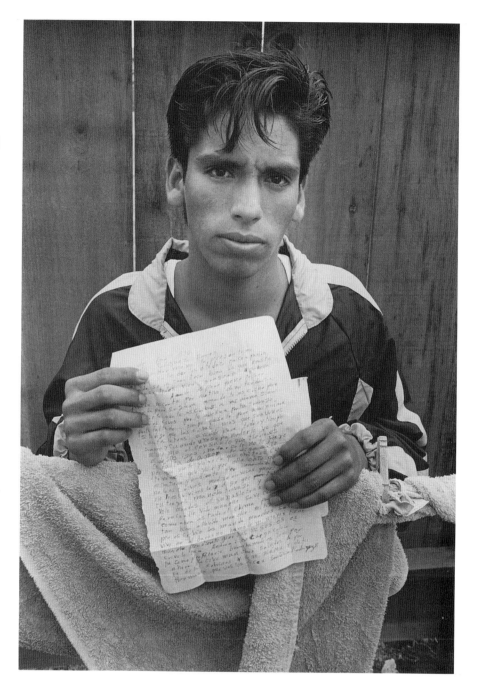

In spite of the closeness in most Mexican farmworker families, many Mexican children often live away from their parents. The reasons are numerous. Parents who follow the crops might leave their children with relatives so the children can stay in one school. Or parents who work in the U.S. might wait to have their family with them until they can afford it or until they can obtain U.S. residency. Or parents might choose to stay in Mexico but have their children live in the U.S. without them, to obtain the best education possible.

Sixteen-year-old Jesús Rodríguez has been living away from his parents and home for over three years. He moved to the U.S. to get a better education and lives with his older brother, Amado, who works in the lettuce fields.

I decided to come to the United States to study and to learn English. I live with my brother Amado in Salinas, California, and my sister Ubaldina lives nearby. We share a house with another family. I like it here, but for living I like it better in Mexico. You don't notice the days here; they pass quickly. But the life there is happier, and most of my family still live there. The Mexican family should always be united, and when it isn't, you feel bad. When the family is together, you can focus on other things besides the fact that the family is separated. You can concentrate in school better if you don't have to worry that your family lives far away.

I used to live on a *rancho* in Nayarit, Mexico, with my parents, brothers and sisters, another family, and my *padrino* [godfather]. My aunts and uncles lived near us. I have two brothers and a sister that still live in Mexico. My father worked in the fields planting corn and pineapples. But he hasn't lived with us since my parents separated. I'd like to see him again. I haven't talked to him in three years.

So now my mother lives alone in Nayarit. It is hard to take care of her because she is far away. She has had problems with her eye — cataracts. They couldn't operate because the eye was very inflamed, and she might lose her sight. She likes where she lives and never said she wanted to go to the United States. I miss my mother because she always treated us well. My mother didn't want me to leave home; she was sad. My father didn't even know that I went away.

The first place I lived without my family was Puerta Vallarta, Mexico. I went there alone and registered for *secondaria* [junior high] by myself. I went to school during the day, and I worked as a *maletero* [bellhop] at night. I sent money home to my mother and visited her by bus every two weeks.

Then I decided to come to the United States. I came over the border with two friends. Another friend who is legal in the U.S. took us to the border. We walked across alone, not with a coyote. I was smiling as I crossed. It seemed incredible to me. It felt like a movie or a dream. Where we crossed, there was wire; now there is a wall there. We saw a lot of trucks with *migra* [immigration agents] inside, and there were no trees to hide in. After we ran and got lost, we hid when we saw a

Jesús talking to Amado at their house

68

helicopter. Some friends were waiting on the other side of the border. We had to leave them at the immigration check in San Clemente. We got lost from them, so we started walking. We went over hills, the rocks, and the beach. Finally my friends found us on a road near the highway in Santa Ana, which is up near Los Angeles. There I called my brother Amado, and he came to pick me up.

Amado is a good brother. He helps out my mother. He sends her money. He is always taking care of her. He has helped all of us. My mother gave him the responsibility to raise me here. He works in the lettuce fields right now. Sometimes we talk and laugh and enjoy each other's company. But it is different than living in Mexico because there I had more liberty to go around. Nobody scolded me. I did things I wanted for me. I was working more and I had money. Here, if I want to buy something I have to ask Amado. I don't like to be asking for things. If I want, I can talk to my sister Uva, but she wants you to do what she says. If I talk to her about my problems, she doesn't help me. Sometimes she scolds me. She'll ask, "Why did you do that?" She doesn't try to understand me. In Mexico, I could always talk to my mother about my problems. I respect her, and she tells me that she doesn't like me to do bad things. Like the time I was drinking in the house. She got angry and told me she didn't like me to drink. She didn't want me to be like my father, a drunk. She didn't shout or punish me; she just spoke to me. I haven't talked to her by phone or seen her for three years since I came here. We write to each other, and she always gives me advice in her letters. But it would be nice to have her with me.

I miss the things my mother did for me. She always washed our clothes and cleaned the house. Now I have to wash and iron my own clothes. Here, it doesn't feel good when I arrive at the house and no one is home. Nobody misses you when you don't come home. Sometimes the kids from the other family we live with say things to me that they shouldn't, but I don't tell them that is is bad to say them because they are not my little brothers and sisters. It's difficult. It's nice to be with a family, to be with someone who loves you, not to be with people you look at for only a short period of time. Sometimes you feel like running. I miss my mother and my home. But at least I live with my brother, instead of alone or with friends.

I have found some good friends here. Some of my friends don't live with their parents. Some are here for their education or they live with a brother, like me, or with one parent, and another parent is working somewhere else. But most of my friends here live with their parents. I don't feel very good that they live with their parents and I don't. Some of their parents are strict, and sometimes they give them permission to do things. On one hand, it is good to have permission so you can enjoy yourself, and on the other hand, something could happen to you.

Some of my friends' parents won't let them go out because of gangs. There are a lot of *cholos* [guys] on the street. Even if you aren't in a gang and you're out

Heading out to a party with friends Salvatore and Federico

Practicing his best stroke, the butterfly

on the streets at night, like the homeboys are, they take you to jail to sleep until the next day. And then if your parents are around, they come and get you. I think the gangs aren't good. Nothing good comes from them. Gangs are why I don't like going to school here.

What I do like about the United States is that there are more opportunities to study and to do what you want, like doing a sport that interests you. I like swimming, so I'm on the team at my school. I swim butterfly, backstroke, and freestyle. But my main reason for being here is that I am studying well. My mother tells me to study, to study a lot. I plan on finishing high school here and then studying in Mexico or maybe here. I want to learn English to help me in the future. Now I don't know a lot of English so they give me lower classes. The students here that know English, and if they are intelligent, get to take the high classes. When I finish high school, I want to study for four years for a *carrera larga*, a profession. I might work as an office manager in a friend's travel agency in Puerta Vallarta. He told me that if I learned English, he would hire me.

I see my future in Mexico, not here. I don't know if I'll live with my mother when I go back to Mexico, but I probably will because it is good to have her near me. It is easier to take care of her, and I wouldn't have to worry as much if she is

Jesús displaying his swim trophy

Relaxing with his niece during a visit from his sister

sick. Even though I like to live on my own and be independent, I like to be with a family, too. I don't know what I'll be doing in the future. It depends on what happens to me. I think my mother is right when she tells me that if I behave well, I'll be something good. If I behave badly, I won't be anyone.

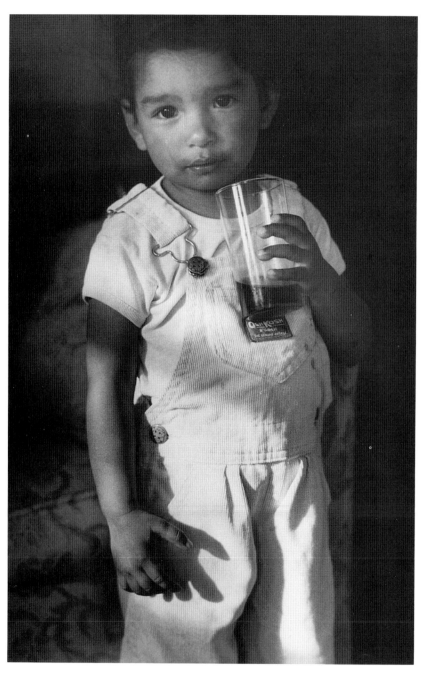

América Reyna, Bonita

A mi hermana chiquita

To my little sister

෨

Como mi hija
te cargué cuidadosamente

como mis lágrimas
te tallé suavemente

como mis fragrantes rosas
olí tu leche haceda

como mis lindas muñecas
te acaricié dulcemente

como mi propio cuerpo
te lavé completamente

Y era joven
y tú eras una bebé

Igual que yo
llevas sangre viva

Igual que yo
el tamaño audaz de nuestros ojos

el color moreno de nuestra piel
nuestras ideas fieras

Oh sweet one,
Reyna, you are more than my sister.

Like my child
I carried you carefully

Like my wet tears
I wiped you softly

Like my fragrant roses
I smelled your spoiled milk

Like my lonely dolls
I caressed you gently

Like my body
I bathed you thoroughly

I was young
You were a baby

Just like me
you carry vivid blood

Just like me
the bold size of our eyes

tanned colored skin
wild ideas

Ay mija,
Reyna, eres más que mi hermana.

Teresa Maturino

Teen Mother

Esmeralda Meza

Children of Mexican farmworkers have a higher pregnancy rate than Anglo-Americans for several possible reasons: most Mexicans are strong Catholics and adhere to the church's stand against abortion and birth control, children often look to develop their own roots somewhere by having a family, and girls in many Mexican farmworker families have traditionally considered their roles to be that of caring for and bearing children. In Monterey County, which includes most of the Salinas Valley, only 30 percent of the population is Hispanic, yet 58 percent of live births are to Hispanic teenage women. Many of these teenage mothers drop out of school to care for their children — increasing the odds that they will end up working in the fields.

Sixteen-year-old Esme Meza lives with her parents, two younger brothers, and her two-year-old daughter, Noemi, in Chualar, California. She is a junior at Alisal High School in Salinas, where she leaves her daughter at the school's day care center. Esme sees Noemi's father most weekends when he comes home from Fresno, California, where he attends college.

My daughter's name is Noemi. She was born when I was fourteen and is an American citizen, like I am. My boyfriend, Ismael — he's nineteen now — is her father. His parents are from Mexico, like mine are, and they work in the fields like mine also. My parents usually work in lettuce, and his parents work mostly in asparagus and celery. Ismael and I used to live together at his parents' house. I had to run away from home to live with him because I didn't have permission to have a boyfriend. Ismael wanted us to go to Planned Parenthood to get birth control. That is when I found out I was pregnant.

I was sort of scared and surprised at the same time when the doctor told me. Ismael was happy, and I knew from the way he responded that he was going to take responsibility. I'm lucky because there are a lot of guys who just leave. I asked him, "How do you feel?" and he said it was O.K. with him to have the baby. Even though I was happy with his answer, I told him that he didn't mind because he wasn't going to have to carry it!

We told Ismael's mother first. I couldn't tell my parents. I tried but I couldn't, so Ismael did when I was three months pregnant. My parents were shocked at first. They had always told me to get on birth control and not get pregnant. Most Mexican parents don't talk about that with their kids. I think that is because they don't communicate. The parents are so tired when they come home from working in the fields. Also, Hispanics don't believe in birth control because they are Catholics and it is against their religion. In other ways, though, our family is just like most Mexican families. We have a different idea about abortion than American families. It seems harder for us to abort or give up for adoption. I think it is also because of our religion and because our families are closer. I think in some American families, if girls get pregnant, they get kicked out, and I didn't. But it always depends on the situation. Because I know some girls whose parents are Mexican like mine, and they beat up on them and said, "Well, you have a baby — it's your problem." And some tell the boyfriend, "Get her out of school. Don't let her go

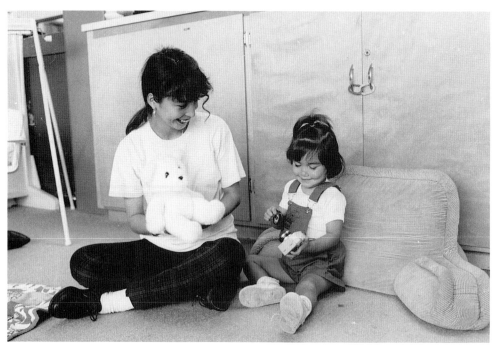

Playing happily with Noemi in day care after school

to school anymore. She has to take care of her baby." For me it was the other way around.

My parents always told us to stay in school because they had to work instead of going to school. I am very fortunate because even though my parents were upset when they first found out I was pregnant, they were more supportive than a lot of parents. Now I'm living at home again with them, and they are helping me.

I was in school during my whole pregnancy. It was my first year of high school. I had nausea at the beginning, and then I was O.K. What was hard was that some kids at school would look at me. They would say hi, but it was to my stomach, not to me. I also would get embarrassed when my friends would walk up to me and rub my stomach. Some people were nice and would ask how I was doing and the baby. But some just would ask, "Are you still with the father?" They didn't really care; they were just being nosy.

Also I was a little nervous about taking care of a baby, because I was too young and in a lot of ways still felt like a child myself. I had helped take care of my little brothers, changing them or giving them a bottle, but I didn't know how to raise a baby. And I felt sort of different from my friends when I was pregnant. They would say let's go to lunch or look at that guy, and I couldn't really get into it. I felt more mature than them. I knew since I was pregnant and was going to have a baby, I couldn't be like them anymore. If any of my friends ever ask me advice when they have a boyfriend, I would tell them to get on birth control right away.

I was in school until May 12, and my daughter was born on May 13. I was really scared and nervous when I had my first labor pains. I didn't know if it was labor or just false labor. I didn't know what was going on. I didn't tell anybody I guess because I was so scared. I wouldn't call the doctor at first, but when I got home, Ismael made me call. By the time I decided to go to the hospital, I was four centimeters dilated. The delivery was hard, but not as hard as people had told me about. It was only three hours and I had heard eight or ten hours. I was so excited to see my baby afterward. There were a lot of people there from our families, so at first I couldn't see her because they were all looking at her! When I finally did, I was really happy. I think I delivered her so fast because I was so anxious to see her.

Noemi is a good daughter, and I have a lot of help with her. Most girls don't, and they have to drop out of school to take care of their babies. They can't afford a sitter, and they don't have anyone to help them. I'm really lucky because there is a day care center at my high school — it's the only one around. At first I thought it was going to be really hard to have my baby. But then I took the course for parenting when I was pregnant and I got into the program. It still is not that easy, but I think I'd be having a lot harder time if I didn't have help and if I was just staying home. I think it is better to get out.

The teacher who runs the center made me feel better when I was pregnant, and she still helps me and all the mothers. She is really great. Now that I've had

Esme and her family with Noemi, who is holding a picture of her father

Noemi and I'm in the day care program, I drop her off in the morning before my regular classes. I'm allowed to see her during the day, but it is difficult for me to leave her. If I do, she cries when I go back to class. I know it is better for her that I don't go and visit her, but I end up missing her a lot also. Usually I don't see her from eight o'clock in the morning until I take my parenting course around three o'clock, after school is over.

The parenting classes really teach you a lot, like how to say no to your child without feeling guilty. After the class is over, I work for my teacher from the center to make some money. I watch the other children who are there or help prepare for the next day's class. So my day is pretty long, and I don't get to do some of the things I used to, like going out with my friends for lunch or anything. Or now if I want to go to the library, where it's easier to study, I can't because I have to take care of my daughter after school.

When I get home, around six o'clock, I have to watch Noemi and my brothers, because my parents are going to school in the evening to learn English. I have to study, and I help out around the house as much as I can. But my whole family helps me and takes care of Noemi, too. My older sister Rosio is really good about taking care of her, and my little brothers play with her. They are too young to do much else. But if I'm at Ismael's house, his brothers are a little older, and they help to change and bathe her. When Ismael is home, he usually just plays and talks to Noemi. He helps out if he sees I need it, but mostly it is all up to me. Sometimes I wish he would help more. I'm lucky that my parents are always helping out.

They also give me advice. They tell me don't be hard on Noemi, she is small and she doesn't know what she is doing. I never hit her, but I have a tendency to yell when she does something. My parents tell me to talk to her straight to her face and tell her what I feel. Then she will understand better. Sometimes I feel badly, because I can't expect my parents to give me all the help I want with Noemi. Like asking them to watch her if they already have a few times that day. Sometimes I want to ask for things but I have to stay quiet because they are doing more than enough for us now. I can't expect more than that from my parents.

They have always been supportive, like with my education. I need to finish school because I have a baby and I have to figure out a way to support her and give her a good life. My parents always told me finishing school was important to make our lives easier. They didn't want me to end up in the fields. They were also encouraging to Ismael. He wanted to drop out of school after I had Noemi to get a job to have more money. He had worked every summer in the strawberry fields and had other jobs, too. His grades were getting worse, but we kept telling him it is better to go to school. Our parents thought it might be harder for them right now if we didn't work but it would pay off in the future. So Ismael started working hard and went to classes after school. And it worked out because now he is in college.

I'm planning on going to college. I didn't used to think about going much until I was pregnant. I wasn't too sure or too motivated. Then I thought I couldn't just drop out of school — I had to think about a baby, too. I wanted to figure out a way to support her and give her a good life. Most of the time Ismael wants me to go to college, but sometimes he tells me that he is going, so I don't need to. I tell him, "What if we don't stay together? Then what am I going to do?" Because you never know what might happen in the future. I want to have a job if we ever get separated, because I don't want to be dependent on him for child support. But I hope we'll be together.

Now we only get to see each other on the weekends, and I miss him a lot and Noemi does, too. When he first went to college, she cried when he left, and then she started crying more when I had to leave her. I think she was afraid that I was going to go away, too. Then I thought she wouldn't recognize Ismael when he came home, but she did. Friends of his at Fresno tell me that when he is up there, he shows pictures of Noemi to everybody. He is really proud of her. This summer we will have a lot of time together because Ismael will be home, and if I'm taking classes, he can spend more time with Noemi and take care of her more.

I don't think we'll be able to see each other as much as I'd like until after we both finish college and start working. That's when we are planning to get married. I wish we could do that now, so we wouldn't have to depend on everybody else. But that is a long time from now. That's also when I would want to have more babies. At least two and maybe up to four. Now since I've had one I know it is difficult to take care of them. But I still want them.

Esme, Noemi, and Ismael playing with one of his puppies

Ismael and I both want to live here, so we can be close to our families, but we want to be able to go to Mexico to visit our grandparents, at least on holidays, like we do now. I want Noemi to have a good education and learn Spanish and English so she knows that she is Mexican and American. I want her to know her great-grandparents and not be ashamed of them, like some Mexicans are who live here. I want her to do what she wants and be happy. I also want her to stay in school and not have too many children. And when she does, she should first be married and have a good career. I don't want her to get pregnant at fourteen, like I did. If someone my age asked me about having a baby when they are a teenager, I would tell them the same thing. It is not that Noemi is so hard to take care of, it's that everything else is harder. But if I could do everything over, I would probably still have her.

Campesinos
Fieldworkers
&

Temprano,
cuando sale el sol,
bultos se mueven por los campos como
relojes en cada amanecer
hasta que la luna sale.

Sus manos de bronce
saludan
como
rifles en una guerra.

Luchando
para sobrevivir
un nuevo mañana
para nuestros hijos. . . .

Los chalecos blancos
de nuestra inocencia
pureza
y riqueza. . . .

Ven niño, deja tu vida sobre la tierra.
Yo soy
el esclavo de mis hijos.

Yo soy
también su dueño.
¡Si!

Yo soy
el campesino
en los campos. . . .

Early,
when the sun comes out,
lumps move throughout the fields like
clockwork every sunrise,
until the moon comes.

Their bronze hands
wave
like
rifles in a war.

Fighting
for survival
a new tomorrow
for our children. . . .

The white vests
our innocence
purity
and wealth. . . .

Come child, leave your life upon the
    land.
I am
the slave of my children.

I am
their owner as well.
Yes!

I am
the *campesino*
in the fields. . . .

Leobardo V. Cortez

Tú Puedes/You Can

꙳

Mari Carmen López

Education is the primary means by which Mexican and Mexican-American farmworker children can have a life different from their parents. Yet 43 percent of the Hispanic population in the U.S. drops out of high school by the age of seventeen. Out of this percentage for Hispanics, Mexican-Americans have the lowest educational level. Even though more Hispanics in California are completing high school than in the past, the children of farmworkers will often work in the fields after high school.

Through the perseverance of teachers, parents, and the students themselves, exemplary schools and programs help these children finish high school and continue on to college. In addition to student programs, those that teach parents how to support their children in school are particularly valuable for farmworkers who did not have the opportunity to finish school. Still, many programs are not extensive enough and are now low on funds.

Eighteen-year-old Mari Carmen López has just graduated from high school. In the fall she will start college at California State University at Fresno, which is not yet a typical accomplishment for farmworker children. Although Mari Carmen and her parents work in the fields, she and, hopefully, her sisters will help to alter these statistics.

I moved to the United States three years ago, when I was fifteen. Until then, I lived in Mexico City with my grandmother and my eight aunts and uncles. When I was a baby, my grandfather, mother, and father moved to America without me because the work opportunities were better. When I was very little, my mother sent my younger sister Jessica, soon after she was born in the U.S., to be with me in Mexico. My mother did that so I would have part of my family with me. I know it was hard for her.

My mother waited until she was a United States citizen to bring me here. She and my father gave me a choice to stay in Mexico or come here. Even though I didn't want to leave my relatives there, I told them that I wanted to come to the U.S. to study. I wanted to be here with my parents, Jessica, and my youngest sister, Ariana. I wanted to learn English because I've always been told that with two languages one can be more prepared. I think that it was a good idea to come here and learn, but I miss my grandmother and her *ánimo* [encouragement]. That is how she and my mother are alike. They always want the best for us. They say to keep on fighting and fighting, until we get the best.

So now I live with my family in Chualar, California, on the property of a lettuce grower. Their lettuce fields are all around us, and my parents work very hard in them. On the weekends, I get up early and work in the fields. Usually I work in the furrows separating the lettuce plants. When I work with a hoe, my back gets sore and it can be a long and very hot day.

My parents feel bad about working in the fields, but they don't have the education to be able to work in anything else. But education is very important to them. They always tell us that we need to go on studying so we don't have to work in the fields. One thing that working in the fields helped me understand is that it is not an easy life and that if you don't study, you'll have to work there. I learned that I need to keep moving forward if I don't want to pass my whole life working in the fields.

When I first came here, it was difficult for me because I didn't understand anything. I had only learned a little English in Mexico. I was a junior then, and some of my homework was in English, so I had to ask my little sister, Ariana, for her help. She was only six then, and I'd have to ask, "How do you say this in English?" and then write it down.

I was very, very nervous my first day at school. I took all my classes in Spanish, except for my class with my ESL [English as a Second Language] teacher. When I finished the first half of the year, I passed to taking my classes in English. My ESL teacher told us there was an after-school program called SCORE that helped students with what they didn't understand in their homework. It was taught by migrant students who had high grades, and I thought that it was a good idea since I didn't understand English or the homework for my classes. I didn't know anybody, but I went because my teacher told me about it.

I think I have different goals from some of the Hispanics that were born here. They have not achieved what I've achieved. I've seen a lot of them drop out of school or get pregnant and have to leave school or get married. They don't see life

Mari Carmen, happy during a visit from her grandmother

like I do. I think they need more information and *apoyo* [support] from their teachers, their parents, and the community.

Ever since we were little, I felt that my parents supported and encouraged us, and not everybody's do. For example, last year this boy I know dropped out of school to work in the fields with his father. My parents always help me, and I think what that boy needed was the encouragement of his parents to stay in school and their confidence in him, so that they all could see he could succeed. My mother has confidence in us and is very involved in the school. She's the vice president of the Migrant Parents Board and has always had close ties with my school.

Also most of my teachers encouraged me to keep studying so I'll be able to

Together with her grandmother and mother

help my parents and have a better future. Really there are many ways in which they help us. If a student really wants to succeed, they can. Like when my ESL teacher gave me the idea to go to Yo Puedo. Yo Puedo means "I Can" in English, and it's a program for migrant farmworkers' children. It takes place in the summer at the campus of the University of California in Santa Cruz. When my teacher saw my grades, she said, "You would qualify to go to Yo Puedo," and I asked her, "What's that?" She said, "Listen, I'm going to go to your house to tell your mother that you qualify for the program," and I said, "Great!" but I still didn't know anything about it. Then she came to talk to my mother, so that's how she helped me. If she hadn't told me about Yo Puedo, I never would have known anything about it.

I wouldn't have been able to go to college if I hadn't gone to Yo Puedo. In the program I studied drama, computers, ceramics, and literature written mostly by Mexicans, some who were migrant farmworkers. We lived in dormitories at UCSC and it was very beautiful because we all lived together. Slowly we all got to know each other, and we became like a family. My favorite class in Yo Puedo was drama because we could express in plays what was going on in real life, like school, or the community, or discrimination. They were like a force. They gave us power. They taught us how to take risks and to rely on each other. We learned to always support each other and say to each other, *"Tú puedes, tú puedes."* So going to Yo Puedo was my first risk and going to Fresno State is the next. It will be hard because I still have obstacles, like English.

Working in the lettuce furrows

Getting a lesson at a Yo Puedo computer class

Even though I think English is important and I need to dominate it before I can succeed, many people here in the United States forget their Spanish and know only English. They lose their roots. In high school, there are kids that don't speak Spanish even though you can tell they are Mexican. At home they speak English. Their parents know English and so they lose their Spanish. I think that's wrong because we need to remember who we are and where we come from and be proud of our culture. They should keep studying in Spanish and keep traditions like celebrating Cinco de Mayo in school. Then they can reflect on and get to know their culture, like they do in Mexico.

I have gained by coming here because I'm learning English and I'm going to college. If I had stayed in Mexico, I wouldn't have learned English. But I don't like the discrimination here. At school, I've seen teachers and counselors telling Spanish speakers to take classes that don't prepare them for college. The classes prepare them more to work right after high school. I don't think that's right. Once a biology teacher told me I should be in a bilingual biology class because she heard me talking to a student in class in Spanish. I told her no because the bilingual biology class is not as difficult as the English class. The biology class in English is also the one I needed to get into college. So I took it, and I ended up getting a better grade than a lot of the students who knew English well.

I like a lot of classes, but biology is my favorite. I like science and want to be a doctor. I'd like to be a pediatrician or a veterinarian. I'd like to be a pediatrician because I'd like to help with a birth, see how a child is born, and help children

Greeting fellow students with the Yo Puedo handshake

and babies when they are sick. Even though I like children, I don't think I'll have them until after I've started my career, so I can give them the education that my parents weren't able to get.

I don't know if I want to be a doctor here in my community or in Mexico. I'm not sure where, but I'd like to have a hospital to help Hispanic people. Fresno State is far away, and it's going to be hard to be away from my family, but because of the goal, it's worth it. I know we'll visit each other and write postcards. Always in my family, they've said how important education is, that not everyone is lucky enough to get one, and that we should always strive for the best.

Tierra Prometida
The Promised Land

ટુ

A los/as estudiantes del
programa Yo Puedo, 1989,
y a sus familias

carguemos con nosotros
siempre nuestras raíces,
enrollémolas para que
nos sirvan de almohada

seamos el sueño
de nuestros antepasados,
la promesa de sus costillas,
la respuesta a sus plegarias

llenemos todas las brechas,
todas las barreras derribemos,
encontremos sagrados
cada rostro, cada árbol

que nuestros oídos oigan
lo que nadie quiere oír,
que nuestros ojos vean
lo que todos quieren esconder

que nuestras bocas hablen
la verdad de nuestro corazón,
que nuestros brazos sean ramas
que a los necesitados den sombra

seamos una llovizna,
la sal de la tierra,
el horizonte que une
el principio y el final

aceptémonos
tal como somos,
tomemos los regalos
y devolvámoslos con creces

veámonos
en veinte años:
quien es ahora la doctora,
la enfermera que cura

quién es ahora el maestro
que de veras enseña
y que de sus alumnos aprende,
la trabajadora social que ayuda

el abogado que defiende
al pobre, al inocente
la organizadora que vuelve
los sueños realidades

quién es ahora madre
que un niño lleva a la escuela,
el amante que perdona
y otra vez vuelve a amar

conservemos para siempre
la criatura que llevamos dentro,
que nos salgan alas en los
    hombros
para que seamos mariposas

seamos la llave que abre
nuevas puertas a nuestra gente
que mañana sea hoy,
ayer nunca se ha ido

demos en este instante
el primer paso:
por fin lleguemos
a nuestra Tierra Prometida!

To the students of the Yo
Puedo program, 1989, and
their families

let us carry our roots
with us all the time
let us roll them up and
use them as our pillow

let us be the dream
of our elders,
the promise of their ribs,
the answer to their prayers

let us fill up all gaps,
tear down all barriers,
let us find godliness
in every face, every tree

may our ears hear
what nobody wants to hear,
may our eyes see
what everyone wants to hide

may our mouths speak up
the truth of our hearts,
may our arms be branches
that give shade to the needy

let us be a drizzle,
the salt of the earth,
the horizon that unites
the beginning and the end

let us accept ourselves
the way we are,
let us take presents in
and give them back manifold

let us see ourselves
twenty years from now
who is now the doctor,
the nurse who can heal

who is now the teacher
who can really teach
and learn from students,
the social worker who cares

the lawyer who defends
the poor, the innocent,
the organizer who makes
dreams come true

who is now the mother
that takes a child to school,
the lover that can forgive
and love again

let us keep forever
the child within each of us,
may our shoulders grow wings
so we can be butterflies

let us be the key that opens
new doors to our people,
let tomorrow be today,
yesterday has never left

let us all right now
take the first step:
let us finally arrive
at our Promised Land!

Francisco X. Alarcón

95

Suggested Reading 🍂

Cockroft, James D. *Outlaws in the Promised Land: Mexican Immigrant Workers and America's Future*. New York: Grove/Weidenfeld, 1986.

Coles, Robert. *Children of Crisis, Vol. 2: Migrants, Sharecroppers, Mountaineers*. Boston: Little, Brown, 1973.

————. *Children of Crisis, Vol. 4.: Eskimos, Chicanos, Indians*. Boston: Little, Brown, 1977.

Daniels, Roger. *Coming to America: A History of Immigration and Ethnicity in American Life*. New York: HarperCollins, 1990.

Farmworkers Justice Fund. *Occupational Health of Migrant and Seasonal Workers in the U.S.* Washington, D.C.: Farmworkers Justice Fund, 1986.

Grebler, Leo et al. *Mexican-American People: The Nation's Second Largest Minority*. New York: Free Press, 1970.

Jiménez, Francisco. "The Circuit." In *Cuentos Chicanos*, Rudolfo Anaya and Antonio Márquez. Albuquerque: University of New Mexico Press, 1984.

Levy, Jacques. *Cesar Chavez: Autobiography of La Causa*. New York: Norton, 1975.

McWilliams, Carey. *California, the Great Exception*. 1949. Reprint. Westport, Conn.: Greenwood, 1971.

————. *Factories in the Fields*. Boston: Little, Brown, 1939.

————. *North from Mexico: The Spanish-Speaking People of the U.S.* 1968. Reprint. Westport, Conn.: Greenwood, 1990.

Meier, Matt S., and Feliciano Rivera. *The Chicanos: A History of Mexican Americans*. New York: Hill & Wang, 1972.

Mirandé, Alfredo, and Evangelina Enríquez. *La Chicana: The Mexican-American Woman*. Chicago: University of Chicago Press, 1979.

Samora, Julian, and Patricia V. Simon. *A History of the Mexican-American People*. Notre Dame, Ind.: University of Notre Dame Press, 1977.

Servin, Manuel P. *A Minority Awakening: The Mexican-Americans*. Mission Hills, Calif.: Glencoe Press, 1970.

Verardo, Jennie, and Denzil Verardo. *The Salinas Valley: An Illustrated History*. Chatsworth, Calif.: Windsor Publications, 1989.

Vigil, James Diego. *Barrio Gangs: Street Life and Identity in Southern California*. Austin: University of Texas Press, 1988.

For Younger Readers

Ashabranner, Brent. *Dark Harvest*. New York: Putnam, 1985.

Blue, Rose. *We Are Chicano*. New York: Franklin Watts, 1973.

Dobrin, Arnold. *The New Life/La Vida Nueva*. New York: Dodd Mead, 1971.

Hewett, Joan. *Hector Lives in the United States Now*. New York: Lippincott, 1990.

Pinchot, Jane. *The Mexicans in America*. Minneapolis: Lerner Publications, 1973.

Roberts, Maurice. *Cesar Chavez and La Causa*. Chicago: Childrens Press, 1986.